Time For Success

How to Build Wealth through Motivation and Entrepreneurship

Charles Lamont

Disclaimer

The information contained in this book is strictly for educational purpose only. The content of this book is the sole expression and opinion of its author and not necessarily that of the publisher. It is not intended to cure, treat, and diagnose any kind of disease or medical condition. It is sold with the understanding that the publisher is not rendering any type of medical, psychological, legal, or any other kind of professional advice. You should seek the services of a competent professional before applying concepts in this book. Neither the publisher nor the individual author(s) shall be liable for any physical, psychological, emotional, financial, or commercial damages, directly or indirectly by the use of this material, which is provided "as is", and without warranties. Therefore, if you wish to apply ideas contained in this book, you are taking full responsibility for your actions.

Table of Contents

Introduction

What would you do if I told you that you could easily build wealth? That's right! You can become a self-made millionaire, as long as you are fully motivated and are willing to work hard for it. Any individual, including yourself, is able to bring in a large amount of money and live the lifestyle they have always dreamed of. Mind you, when I talk about being motivated, I'm not talking about wanting money – that's not true motivation.

Every person out there wants MORE money, right? The difference between wanting money and being motivated by money involves the willingness to take the necessary actions in order to make it.

You see, when an individual tells me that they want more money, I noticed they aren't willing to do the work that is needed. They want to live that lavish lifestyle, but they are not willing to wake up early and work late until the sun goes down.

They want to put in as little hours as possible so that they can spend time at home or on vacations. Sure, those type of people can make money, but they aren't going to become multimillionaires.

If you are looking for secrets to becoming a multimillionaire without putting in a large amount of work, you have come to the wrong place … the wrong place is planet Earth, because there is no such thing as becoming a millionaire without hard work, unless you win the lottery.

Becoming a millionaire is all about doing the jobs that others stay away from. It is about getting on airplanes, getting up early, staying up late, missing your family and putting a lot of thought into your work.

The more people you reach out to and serve, the more money you are going to make. The more people that benefit from the company you have created, the more money you will earn.

If you want money, you're never going to have it, unless you're lucky. You have to be motivated enough to push yourself to wake up early and work long hours – you have to be motivated to work harder than others. If you are willing to do all this, money will find its way to you.

Are you doing all you can do in order to produce the financial results you desire? What could you do in order to create more value for people? Are you truly motivated?

Unless you are fully motivated, you're not going to be the successful entrepreneur you need to be. If you're not motivated, you're not going to be successful at all!

I believe it's time for you to learn how to build wealth through motivation and entrepreneurship, which is why I decided to write this book in the first place. In this book, I am going to teach you the anatomy of an entrepreneur, tell you why money isn't the root of all evil, and share some secrets with you and more.

1: The Anatomy of a Successful Entrepreneurship

I would like to start out by taking a look at the anatomy of a successful entrepreneurship because I believe this is important. In order to have a successful entrepreneurship, you must understand the anatomy behind it. Correct?

Most entrepreneurs have a goal. They want to control their own destinies and that is one of the biggest reasons why they try to start their own business. This desire is so strong that entrepreneurs risk their future and careers simply to be their own boss.

They are not fully fulfilled until they are the boss – they're not happy following someone else's plans, knowing they too could develop plans of their own. Many times, these individuals believe they have ideas that would revolutionize their industry and they are probably right about that.

So, let's take a close look at the anatomy of a successful entrepreneurship …

Confidence

Through research that has been conducted, we have found that successful entrepreneurs share similar personality trails, with confidence being one of the most important. When I mention confidence, I'm not just talking about confidence within themselves, I am talking about confidence in their ability to set up a business, sell their ideas and run with their intuition. There is no denying the facts that running a small business is competitive and it's those business owners with the right amount of confidence who survive.

The Ability to Adapt

Successful entrepreneurs will need to have the ability to adapt. As you start your business, you will discover the very things you expect to work won't work. On the same note, you will come across things you didn't expect to work that will work for you.

You can look at others that are in your industry, see what they are doing and use their ideas. Point blank, successful entrepreneurs have the ability to adapt. Sure, you may start out and be one of those lucky ones whose initial ideas work without any flaws, but trust me; the world is going to change around you.

I have a friend who is a good entrepreneur in my book. He started out as a residential realtor and was doing an excellent job. When the market for home sales collapsed, he transformed his business into property management – the two businesses required similar skills, so why not? Many times, people are forced to morph their own business.

You see, it is important that entrepreneurs are adaptable. As an entrepreneur, the only thing that is going to be constant is change. If you do not adapt, the entire enterprise could be swallowed by the rising tide we know as change.

Work Ethic

Work ethic is another that should be listed as anatomy for a successful entrepreneur. There is no denying the fact that running a small business is going to be hard. You will be dealing with days that are longer than eight hours. There are times when you will start working on a Monday and by Thursday, you will pass 40 hours, but you shouldn't let this slow you down. Running a business means you will be available 24/7.

To be a successful entrepreneur, you must be able to put in hard work – there is nothing lazy in this picture.

Yes, there will be challenges, regardless of the business you are in. As long as you are adaptable and are willing to work extremely hard, you will improve your chances of being successful.

Persistence

There will be times when your favorite employee leaves your company and they may even become your competition. The government may even change regulations, making things harder on you. In order to succeed, you will need to be persistent during those harsh times.

In addition to the willingness to persist, you will need the financial means to persist. You'll need a cash reserve that will see you through the lean times. When considering the launch of a business, assume that everything will take twice as long and cost twice as much as you expected. If you can't afford this, delay the launch of your enterprise. Conservatism in the planning stage is often a lifesaver down the road.

If you are looking to build wealth through entrepreneurship and motivation, you definitely need to have the anatomy of a successful entrepreneur. Otherwise, your chances of succeeding are pretty slim. Moving further, let me introduce you to the common characteristics of successful entrepreneurs …

Do What You Enjoy Doing

This is your time to gain wealth through entrepreneurship - it is your time to shine. What good would it do to choose something you don't enjoy doing? If you really want to feel motivation, you need to choose a niche that you enjoy.

Carefully Make Plans

You must plan every aspect of your business, regardless of what it is. Planning everything, when you start your own business, is a habit you must adopt.

Business planning is very important because it requires you to research and compile data, analyze every business situation and make a conclusion based on the facts of your research. Think of your business plan as a second function. This mean you will have your goals and how to achieve your goals written down on paper.

Take Your Work Seriously

You cannot be successful and be effective in business unless you take your job seriously. Far too many fail simply because they weren't serious enough, were easily sidetracked and they did not stay motivated.

Manage Money Correctly

You must be able to manage money correctly because as you know, cash flow, in any business, is the lifeblood. In order to make sure the cash flows continuously and to make sure the bills are paid on time, you must manage your money wisely. I cannot stress this enough!

When it comes to managing money wisely, there are a couple of aspects:

Expenses - The cash you put towards supplies, inventory, rent, wages and other items you need for your business.

Income - The money you make from your clients in exchange for your services and/or goods.

Have a Positive Business Image

When it comes to possible clients, you only have a couple of minutes to make a positive and memorable impression. You will need to go out of your way in order to make an effort to project the most positive business image possible.

Communicate with Your Customers

You must be willing to communicate with your customers. Customers are tired of dealing with automated machines – they want to talk to actual human beings. Be there for your customers and become friends with them.

Be an Expert in Your Field

Whatever field you go into, you need to become an expert. If you go into a field and it is obvious that you're not an expert, you won't make many sales. Think about it – when you're looking for a solution to your problems, you actively look for an expert.

Make it Easy for People to do Business with You

You need to make it as easy as possibly for people to do business with you. Remember, people go out of their way to work hard and give you their hard earned money in exchange for your services. Making it easy for others to do business with you means you will need to make yourself accessible about the products and services you are offering. At all times, you will need to give customers what they want and when they want it.

A Good Reputation

A good reputation isn't something you can buy. A good reputation is something that you will need to earn. You can earn the reputation by pleasing others by keeping your promises. For example, if you promise high quality content, then you must live up to those expectations. If you offer to repair something, you need to fix it and it needs to last.

Attention Grabbers

Knowing how to grab attention will definitely help you out. You cannot waste money, time and energy on promotional activities because you risk the chances of running out of money. Instead, with every promotional activity you take part in, you need to put money back in your pocket so that you can continue to grow your business.

Organizations

As a successful entrepreneur, you cannot be sloppy – you must stay organized. Getting organized isn't all about knowing where your files are, it's also about managing your business. It involves having good systems in place to get things done. You need to develop a routine that will help you accomplish as much as possibly during your workday.

Concentration

You need to have the ability to concentrate on the most important things and stay on track. No success is possible, without being able to concentrate on a single goal or task. The best way to do this is to make a list for each day, then prioritize that list by putting the numbers 1-10 next to each task. Once you have figured out which task is the most important, start with that one and work yourself down.

Courage

This reminds me of one of my favorite quotes by Winston Churchill "Courage is rightly considered the foremost of the virtues, for upon it, all others depend." When it comes to taking entrepreneurial risks that are necessary to become wealthy, it will take a large amount of courage.

Time Off

Yes, you have to work extremely hard in order to get anywhere in this world, but if you work non-stop, without any breaks, before you know it, you'll get burned out.

I highly recommend establishing a regular work schedule that includes a lunch break and time to go out and stretch your legs. You could even schedule a couple of nice vacations in there during the year. So, take it from me, "All work and no play will make you burn out fast and will cause you to be grumpy towards your customers."

Being able to grab attention, having good communication skills, being able to work hard, being able to adjust and everything else I discussed in this chapter is what makes up the anatomy of a successful entrepreneur.

Why Money Isn't the Root of All Evil

Seriously, how many times have you heard "Money is the root of all evil." Honestly, I have heard this more times than I want to hear it. I've even seen it hanging on walls in public. Yes, this is a popular saying, but takes it from me, it certainly isn't true. The Bible says "Love of money is evil." There is a big difference. We all need money to survive. There is nothing wrong with acquiring lots of money if you do it the right way.

Look, if money really was the root of all evil, like some will lead you to believe, there would be people out there who were trying to be as poor as possible. So many people, like you, wouldn't be trying to get rich – because they wouldn't want to be evil.

Do you feel me on that? Yes, there are people of faith who give away a large amount of income in order to help those who are living in poor conditions, but they do that in order to share their wealth and describe it as a special calling.

Even if you are not religious, just stop for a minute and think about the logic behind this popular saying. If money truly was the root of all evil, only those people who had money would be doing evil things, and the people who had the most money would be the most evil of them all.

Yes, people who don't have money like to think this is true, but it really isn't. Poor people can lie, steal, cheat, kill and assault just as well as wealthy people.

Let's take a second to look at this from another angle. Greed can cause people to do some bad things, but so can hatred, jealousy and the desire for revenge.

When a man goes to a bar and drops a drug into a woman's drink, do you think money is on his mind? No, he has something more than money on his mind. He wants to be able to take her home unconscious so he can do bad things.

When I was in a public forum the other day, an individual said "money is the root of all evil" and that right there is what made me want to write this chapter of the book. That individual was using that phrase as an excuse for not saving money. It was almost as if she was saying "I am a better person, because I do not have a lot of money."

However, the way I look at it, going out and intentionally spending all of your money as soon as you make it really doesn't make you a better person, unless, of course, you're giving it away for a good cause. Instead, in my eyes, and in the eyes of many others, this makes you irresponsible.

On another note, making good use of the resources you have and opening a savings account for your future will not make you evil. You will be able to help others if the need ever arises.

I feel that when talking about building wealth through entrepreneurship, I have to point out the fact that money really isn't the root of all evil.

In the world today, there are numerous ways you can build your wealth. You can build your wealth through sports, careers, entrepreneurship or even crime! Obviously there are numerous advantages and disadvantages to each method with crime being fairly self-explanatory.

While there may be many risks associated with becoming an entrepreneur, as long as you learn from your mistakes and persist, you will eventually become successful. The freedom of being your own boss and the chance to make significant financial gain as an entrepreneur is a choice many people can only dream about.

Point blank, either way you stack it, regardless of how you put it, money really isn't the root of all evil. I just wish this phrase would stop popping up every time I turn around because it couldn't be further from the truth. After reading this chapter, I hope that you have a clear understanding that money is not the root of all evil.

3. Ways to Build Wealth Faster

When you first start out, wealth isn't just going to knock on your door – this is something that will take time. Sure, back in the day, while sitting in my chair, I wished money would just come and knock on my door, but it never did and that is when I decided I had to get up out of that chair and do something about it.

Yes, I understand you want to speed the process up and I am willing to share some of my secrets you could use in order to build wealth faster.

To start with, you need you to realize what wealth is. When talking about wealth, I'm not exactly talking about money. Mind you, I don't look at wealth as being the same as money. Wealth, believe it or not, is as old as human history. In fact, thinking about it, plants have wealth …money is actually a recent invention.

You see, I view wealth as being a fundamental thing. Wealth involves stuff we want: clothes, cars, food, houses, vacations, technology, and so on. You can have wealth without having any money. You see, if you were magic, you could create that car of your dreams or that house of your dreams.

With magic, you could create anything your heart desired and you wouldn't need money! Whereas, if you're in the middle of nowhere, where there are no stores and you have no connection to the Internet, it wouldn't matter how much cash you had.

Basically, what it all boils down to is, wealth is about what you want, not money. However, why is everyone talking about making money? Well, in all actuality, money is a way of moving wealth. Most of the things you need, you won't be able to make yourself – if you want a place to live, you will need to get it from someone else.

So, how do you get the person who built that house to give it to you? By giving that person something in return … by giving them money. You won't get that house, unless you give that person something they could use and we could all use money.

Yes, we could all use money … so, what can we do in order to build wealth faster?

If you really want to build wealth faster, you need a plan of action. Go ahead and use these steps to build wealth faster …

1. Figure out exactly what you want in life and write it down.

2. Develop clear goals – make sure they are measurable and specific.

3. What is the most important skill you could learn that would help you move to the top in your niche? Do something to learn those skills.

4. Is there a major constraint that is limiting you from achieving success as a successful entrepreneur? Eliminate it.

5. Do you have a big obstacle in your personal or business life? Focus your time on possible solutions to getting over that obstacle. You won't be able to move forward until that obstacle has been eliminated.

6. Make a list of what you would like to do.

7. Realize that you are responsible for what goes on in your life. Don't make excuses or blame others for every negative event that happened in your life. Instead, take action in order to take your goals and transform them into reality.

8. Visualize your goals of excellent health and financial success. During this time, remember, the person you see in the mirror is the person you are going to be.

There are few ways to build wealth through business ownership. You can pay yourself an increasingly larger salary as you build a business organically or through acquisition. You can then monetize the value of the business you have created by transitioning ownership or selling the business in whole or part.

In the first way of building wealth, you work hard and hopefully watch the business grow. As your profits grow, so does your salary. Eventually, you may be able to take home a few hundred thousand each year and still maintain complete ownership.

In the second way of building wealth, people have literally made millions and tens of millions; this typically entails strategic growth and ultimately selling the company. You should bear in mind that there is a huge potential to make a lot of money in selling a business compared to running it.

The first way to build wealth is fairly simple, you need to build a business and pay yourself first. If your business continues to grow and can pay your salary, you can re-invest some of the money back into your company.

Doing this method can earn you six figure salary every year while you still maintain majority ownership. You will still have time to enjoy other commitments such as with your family, friends, and the community you live in. This method of becoming wealthy is often associated with the lifestyle of an entrepreneur and large business owners, or small corporations.

If making a six figure income every year doesn't satisfy you, and you wish to make tens or even hundreds of millions dollars per year, then maybe the second option is for you. In order to make this kind of money, you will need to change you thinking, goals and methodology. Obviously, most people can't even get close to achieving this kind of goal.

You will need to build a massive company from ground up. You will need to fill a large market in order to make your business successful. In order to use this method you will have to be an elite entrepreneur or a large corporation. You will have to develop and manage top of the line newest technology, obtain solid foundation, have business plan that is exceptional, fill the market need, have outstanding customer service, and the business must be fail proof.

Your complete business plan must be very powerful and convincing so that you will be able to find private investors and venture capitalists to help with the funding and to invest with your company.

In return, they would own a certain percentage of your company and earn dividends or the percentage of the profit the company earns.

You will need to hire the best, most qualified candidates to run your corporation. You may have to give up additional portions of your ownership to fill this need. You will have to find additional products or services to market and to build a new team that can process outsourcing.

What I have explained above is at the basic level of how the system works. Being able to go public with your business or selling a company is a goal many potential entrepreneurs dream about.

If you can start with a product that the market demands, establish market share, build a good team, add additional products and revenue streams, turn profits and establish yourself as a market leader in your niche, you will have all the tools required to make it.

This process is extremely difficult and has a higher risk. Even the most experienced entrepreneurs fail to succeed following this path. However, if they do succeed, the rewards are massive.

There is nothing wrong with becoming wealthy through the cash flow of a small business. It all becomes a valuable experience on how to start your own business.

Like anything, the steps outlined above takes time and are challenged with many difficulties. I am now going to outline how to build a million dollars a year business.

Most people will go their entire lives without earning millions, so for me to tell you that some businesses reach this milestone in one year might sound crazy. However, it is possible and plenty of businesses have achieved this goal in the past.

The first step you need to take is to find a growing market, one of the easiest ways to build a million dollar company in such a short space of time is to find a growing trend and ride it all the way to the top.

A great example is by someone named Micah Adler, who just so happens to be the CEO of mobile app developer Fiksu.

This grew from less than one million dollars to over 100 million dollars in just three and a half years following its 2010 launch. The amazing thing about this success story is that it only started with 17.6 million dollars in venture capital. Part of Adler's success obviously came from building great products, although a great deal came from timing.

Just two years after Fiksu's launch in 2012, mobile-app development represented 19 billion dollars in revenue and was experiencing annual growth of more than 60 percent a year. If you find a growing market of your own like, this will put you on the fast track to massive revenue growth.

The second step you need to take is to think monetization from the start. This may sound strange but some start-ups start without any obvious monetization strategies, twitter being an obvious example.

Most profitable companies operate from one of two models: they either sell a lot of inexpensive products to a lot of people or they sell more expensive products to fewer people.

Both models have their merits, although it is imperative you have a devised plan for monetization. Knowing how you will make money from the start will prevent wasted time hoping that something profitable will magically come together for you.

The third step you need to take is to make sure you are the best.

There are plenty of mediocre products out there, although to be honest you can safely assume they are not making a millions in their first year. If you want to hit massive potential profits quickly you have to bring something to the table that wows customers and generates a buzz and interest in your market place.

How can you tell if you have a "hot product? Simple really, if you are not getting rave online reviews or positive comments, it is highly unlikely that your clients are ecstatic about your product as you predicted to be.

Asking your customers what you can do to make your existing product better will go a long way to getting them to refer further sales for you in the future, in turn growing your company further.

Hitting one million in revenue in one year is no small feat and there is no way you are going to hit this goal if you hire a team of underperformers.

Of course, hiring these kinds of people will be cheaper and easier, but you'll pay the price when your end-of-the year sales number comes up short. Instead you should hire a great team and the best way to do this is to ask around for referrals.

You should particularly pay attention to the sales hiring as these key employees will make the biggest difference to your businesses. You should encourage them to do whatever is necessary to close the deal. A useful tip to motivating your workforce is the fact that a series of incentives can go a long way.

Finally, if you shoot for the revenue moon (i.e. One million in one year) you need to be completely militant on gathering data and acting on it. When approaching a new product, work in short increments of few weeks or less to try something new, check the statistics to see how the changes impacted revenue, and then depending on the outcome, apply the changes or try a new experiment.

If you want to build wealth through entrepreneurship and start your own business, a massive factor that will ultimately influence the success of your business is "branding." Branding plays such a massive role for small businesses as it does for larger ones.

Indeed a trick bigger firms employ is to look more like a small firm in order to appeal to consumers that prefer to support independent brands. There is a crucial link between successful businesses and strong branding.

Branding is a way of defining your business to yourself, your team and your external audiences. If your brand embodies the core of what your business is and its values it helps define your business identity. Customers today are savvy enough to see through most attempts by companies to spin, gloss or charm their way to sales.

The huge benefit a strategically defined brand can bring is the same as when people fall in love with each other. A customer will connect with a brand because they share the same values and beliefs of the brand. When your brand can connect emotionally with other people, it will lead to higher sales and a better brand differentiation.

Define your brand by reviewing the product or service your business offers, pinpoint its space in the market and research the needs and concerns of your customers. A successful brand will promote the business, connect with its customer base and differentiate itself in the market at the same time.

When you build your brand you should think of it as a person and consider what is driving your business. What does your brand believe in and what is its purpose?

Of course, none of these things are going to happen, unless you are motivated. Pay attention to the next chapter because I am going to give you some of my secrets to staying motivated.

4. How to Become Motivated

Yes, I understand, it is one thing to read about being motivated, but it's another to actually become motivated. Being motivated means you stick around with your business in spite of the challenges that come your way and trust me, there's going to be some challenges - you just need to learn how to overcome those challenges.

Whether you are involved in a trade selling a product or a company offering certain services, it is quite easy for you to stay motivated when business is good and the cash is flowing. But when failures strikes, how do you deal with it?

Today, I would like to take time to share my thoughts on how to become motivated when starting your own business and how to stay encouraged when the going gets tough.

Find Your Passion

To become motivated, anyone who is just starting a business should consider a product he or she uses and patronizes. For example, if you have someone who despises cooking, it wouldn't make sense for them to create a cook book or a recipe site, would it?

In an article he wrote for Forbes Entrepreneurs called " What Motivates Successful Entrepreneurs?," Alex Lawrence, the founder of Startup Flavor, claimed that he wanted to share his product with people so the customers will have a chance to experience and appreciate the product the same way that he did. After all, you have already risked your time and money; you might as well have faith in what you are doing.

If it's a service-oriented company, consider something that you would love to do over and over again for your clients. In other words, find your passion and build your business with your passion as your foundation. In the same article, Lawrence also mentioned that being an entrepreneur actually relates to being happy in giving service to people.

Envision Your Business' Potential

To stay motivated, it would also help to envision the potential of your business. Adam Fridman, founder of MeetAdvisors, believed that "Every great entrepreneur had a vision of what they wanted to achieve, and for good reason - it's unbelievably motivating" (Fridman, 2015).

Think of what you want to do with your trade or enterprise. Dream it and work on it. If it is a product, do you intend to sell it to young professionals, adults in their thirties or forties, senior citizens or there is no preferred age group? Do you think your product will be a hit among women, men or both genders?

If it is a service, are you going to rent a space or work from home? Based on the nature of the service, would you prefer if customers come to you or will you offer home service?

Set Your Goals

I am a firm believer in setting your goals. If you want to achieve anything, you must have something to aim for. It is important to identify your goals for your enterprise. It is best to identify your short-term plans as well as your long term targets.

Whichever it is, it is most important that your goals are realistic, or you might be disappointed in the end. In her "3 Ways to Stay Motivated to Lead Your Business," Deborah Mitchell elaborated that it is better to "set several smaller, measurable milestones so that you can track your progress."

This way, it would be easier and faster for you to tick off a bullet from your list of goals and you'll feel better regarding the status of your venture.

After all, you'll still get there even if you're just taking baby steps.

Check On Your Progress

As mentioned above, keeping track of the growth of your enterprise will make you feel good. As Fridman puts it, realizing how much development your business has gone through will give you enough motivation.

But don't stop there. Again, Fridman pointed out that every failure should be seen as a lesson. Identify what went wrong and improve it. Every entrepreneur should reflect on how to make their merchandise or service even better to keep their clients.

Get Some Well-Deserved R&R

You worked hard. You gave your all to make your business succeed and now it's time to play harder. Don't burn yourself out by working all day, every day. Take some time off, as both Fridman and Mitchell advised.

It could be as simple as spending some time with your family or friends. It could even be just picking up on an old hobby like reading books or watching TV shows, Mitchell recommended. But it would be better if you do it regularly, as it "gives your brain time to rest, recalibrate and be ready to run a successful business."

For Fridman, he believed that a good R&R "allows for a proper return to form the next day" That vacation, short or long, may be just be what you need to renew your passion.

Finding Motivation When You're Depressed

I feel the need to cover this topic because it only seems right, since there are so many people who have been diagnosed with depression. Telling a depression person that they need to get motivated is almost like telling a kitchen utensil to run away with the spoon - you will get the same result.

Mind you, this isn't because depressed people do not want to get motivated, it is because being motivated is overwhelming to them. Motivation isn't impossible – you just need to find that one process that works for you.

Here's a technique you can try if you are depressed …

Every morning, when you get out of bed, try to perk up as much excitement as you possibly and force it out of your body. Don't give yourself any time to sit there and dwell. Get dressed as soon as you get up.

Get dressed up, do your hair, make yourself attractive (if you are a female) and get all of this done quickly. Don't give yourself any time to talk yourself out of it. Getting dressed and making yourself look attractive is a good motivation to get you moving in the right direction every day. It is also great for alleviating depression.

If you are taking the day off, go walk the dog, go to the gym, go out into the yard and do some yard work for about 30 minutes or so. Whatever you do, go out and enjoy the sunshine. Did you know that spending at least 20 minutes out in the sun on a daily basis will lift your mood?

If you are not able to get up and find motivation to do anything, please don't sit there and berate yourself for this. You're still up and ready to start your day, right? Let go of those major expectations and live life to the fullest. Focus on the positive things you have done. The trick is not to be too hard on yourself. Don't make getting motivated feel like such a chore.

Depression will speak to you – it will say "you can't do anything right," "Why aren't you further along in your career" or "look what you've done with your life." Don't listen to any of those things.

Replace these phrases with positive phrases in order to change your way of thinking. By doing this, you will be creating a neural pathway in your brain.

To create those new neural pathways, all you have to do is generate positive thoughts about yourself. Over time, before you know it, the bad pathways will die like leaves on a flower. All you need is some determination and you will be on the right path.

Socializing is Important

When it comes to motivation, you cannot leave socialization out of the picture. You need to schedule appointments with your family and friends. If you don't have any family or friends, don't use it as an excuse.

You can go to the bookstore where there are people – this is better than sitting at home alone. Who knows, by going out in a public area, you might just make some new friends. That, in my book, is motivating.

Give Yourself Credit

Even if the task you have done is tiny, if you are proud of it, give yourself credit. Do you have 2 piles of paperwork to fill out? Tell yourself you will fill that pile of paperwork in about an hour, then go ahead and finish the job set out to do. Don't procrastinate! You will be surprised at how much you accomplish by taking this route.

Many people struggle with being motivated and when you're depressed, it is even more of a struggle. Remember, you are not alone.

To truly become motivated, you need to take the first step and never look back. Find what works with you, and from there, the motivation will continue. I know, again, it is not easy, but with practice, you can accomplish this and then it will become easier.

5. What Will Real Success Look Like?

True success as an entrepreneur may be different for everyone. Reaching a certain number of employees, hitting a specific amount of sales, purchasing a dream car, living in a dream home, having a large amount of money in a bank and being able to provide for the family are some of the things associated with success.

Upon hearing the phrase "true success," many individuals will automatically have visions of vacations, big parties, a mansion; a large amount of money and so on… and there is nothing wrong with this.

Honestly, I could never have imagined anyone complaining about having too much money, but when Markus Persson (the Minecraft creator) sold his rights to the game to Microsoft, he must be the first.

He has been complaining about having too much wealth and this wealth has led to depression. He complains, because it's awkward hanging out with his normal friends, he has to wait for his normal friends to get off work and he feels like he has reached the top, so there's no part in trying anymore.

As an entrepreneur, if you ever run into this problem, don't look at it as if you're at the top, because you are never truly at the top, not when there's so much more inventions that can be done. What I'm saying is once you master one thing, you can move to the next. This way, your "true success" will never come to an end and you will never feel lousy or depressed about it.

When an individual thinks of true success, they also think of having that impressive job title, wearing proper clothes, having the perfect body, working long hours and, of course, being respected by every other person on the planet.

Many put in long hours at a job that they think will bring in the most money. Each time their pay goes up, so does their standard of living. Once they are in a different league, the vacations become more exotic than ever before and their cars get fancier too. In an effort to show others that we are successful, we may overextend ourselves – we may become stressed and even over exhausted.

With all that said, tell me this – does THAT sound like true success? I'd have to say "no."

So, the question still remains – what does true success look like? True success is your face on the cover. True success means you are doing exactly what you were meant to do on this planet.

True success involves doing what you feel and having fun while doing it. It is realizing the fact that you were put on this planet for a reason. As a result, you will begin to recognize the value in every person and you will take better care of yourself.

Move forward and you will be rewarded both financially and emotionally. Here are some truly successful entrepreneurs:

- Cesar Millan
- Oprah Winfrey
- Buddy Valestro

Wouldn't you like to add your name to this list? Well, their careers worked for them, because they were born to do it. Take Cesar Millan as an example, he was raised around pit bulls and loves the breed, so he was born to rescue them and be labeled "The Dog Whisperer."

Each and every single successful entrepreneur serves the world with their gifts and talents, and so can you. Think about what you enjoy doing and make that part of your everyday life. This will give you the motivation to strive and move forward with your plans.

Even when others are not aware of it, you need to have courage to see that the things you have in your life truly are precious. Learn to let go of perfection and take on your life exactly as it was meant to be. Financial success, in my opinion, should simply be a nice by-product, not a goal in itself.

Now, I'd like to talk about your business vision …

What's Your Business Vision?

Surely, you have a business vision? If you don't have one, write it down now. Mind you, the vision you have right now of your company could change as time goes by. Come up with an idea of what your business will feel, look and act like the future, when it is steadily running. I like having a clear vision, because this is what gives me the opportunity to define success.

Do you need help writing that business plan? Okay, let me help you with that. Sit down and envision your business five years from now. Start writing as if you are writing a story about your business – explain everything from the look of your room to the pictures hanging on the wall. You can talk about the atmosphere, people sitting in front of you, the products/services and the revenues – everything.

Now, do you see what real success looks like? By now, you probably have a whole different picture in your mind when it comes to success and that may be a good thing, especially if the only thing you thought of when you dreamed of success was that lavish lifestyle.

6. Secrets of Self-Made Millionaires

Now that you have an idea of what true success looks like, let's move forward and talk about some secrets of self-made millionaires. Perhaps someday you will get the chance to be in their shoes one day – maybe not today or tomorrow, but one day.

To start, if you truly want to make millions, it is important that you realize you no longer want to be just a millionaire – you want to BECOME a multimillionaire. Does that make sense?

Yes, I understand, you can make a million dollars and right now, you feel as if this is going to give you financial security. However, I'm sorry to break it to you, but it will not give you the financial security you need. Look at the volatility in the economy and the financial markets throughout the world. We can no longer say that being a millionaire will help us provide for our families with real security.

I'm not giving you a "how-to" on pinching pennies – these secrets I am going to give you are about making multimillion dollar wealth and enjoy making it. Check out these secrets …

Number 1 - Decide to BE a millionaire

The first step to having a lot of money involves deciding to be a self-made multimillionaire. There is one millionaire I know that went from having nothing to being where he is today. While he started out with nothing, he did have lots of great ideas. He was able to create a net worth that cannot be destroyed in one lifetime. The first step he took was making a decision and then setting a target.

Number 2 - Treat it Like Work

How do you think self-made millionaires made it to the top? They didn't get there just by sitting there with no motivation! You need to be fully motivated, not just about making money, but in every aspect of your life.

You see, I have always wanted a large amount of money and that desire was driven by my need to contribute on a consistent basis with my potential. When things get rough, millionaires don't run inside, they find a way to get through the storm. They do this because they see the difference they can make within their company, families, charities and community.

Number 3 - Stop Thinking About Poverty

We're not running out of money on Earth – we are running out of people who are not thinking correctly. Eliminate the poverty thinking. I am telling you this because it is what I had to do. I was raised by a family who didn't have a whole lot of money to spare – we could barely pay our bills every month, let along afford food.

Many of the lessons I learned as a child gave me a sense of fear and insecurity. Can you blame me? I was continuously told to eat all of my food, because there were people out there who didn't have enough food to eat. I was told not to waste anything, because money didn't grow on trees. I am sure many of you have heard these same phrases over and over again as you were growing up. With such thinking, wealth and abundance cannot be created. So, you have to stop thinking about poverty.

Number 4 - Get to Know millionaires

Ever since I was a kid, I wanted to learn about wealthy people. They were very interesting to me. I loved reading about their work, their lavish lifestyle and all of that other stuff that comes with being a millionaire. I enjoyed reading their book to find out all the struggles they went through in their life and the turning point to their success I This really inspired me to follow the same path.

You see, you cannot learn how to make large amount of money from someone who don't have a lot of money – that just wouldn't make sense. If they have the secrets to making a large amount of money, why aren't they rich? I'm sure you get the picture here.

Who is well-known for saying this phrase "Money doesn't make you happy." Can you guess? People without money! Rich people don't normally use such phrases – there's no need to. You need to look into these millionaires (there's thousands of them out there) and see what they are doing and follow their footsteps.

For example, how do they invest? What do they like to read? How do they stay motivated to move forward? What excites them the most? What gives them the most power? In order to become a millionaire, you will first need to get to know them and think like them.

Number 5 - Work As If You Are Already a Millionaire

Millionaires look at the clock differently. Instead of glancing up at the clock, they buy it and people who are living in poverty sell it. You need to start buying that clock.

You see, rich people understand that time is more valuable than money and with that in mind, they reach out and hire people to do the things that they are not good at, like writing, or they hire maids to do their household chores, because they know cleaning is not a productive use of their time.

Many people sit on their couches and say "Those wealthy people have money handed to them." That is not always true. Wealthy people, unless they inherited their money somewhere down the line, worked hard to get where they are today and you could do the same thing.

Those individuals who are financially successful are fully motivated and are continuously hunting for success and working hard to get there. They are not just sitting there talking about other people – other people really aren't even on their agenda.

Number 6 – Have Multiple Flows of Money

People who are really rich never actually depend on one source of income. One of the steps to becoming a self-made millionaire involves creating multiple flows of income.

By doing this, you will have money coming in different directions and if one fails, you will be able to rely on the other. For example, I have a friend who created a consulting business, along with a real estate business and once that once they became unproductive, he moved on to creating a web design business.

Number 7 – Don't Spend Your Money

When people start to make more money than they are used to, naturally they start spending it and this is poor money management. Millionaires are not out there spending their money even though they are able to.

Instead, they are investing it. They understand that the tax laws in the United States favor investing over spending. When you go out and buy a house, you won't be able to write it off. Instead, the rich go out and purchase something, like an apartment, which will produce a nice cash flow for them and they can write it off year after year.

You see, you go out and purchase cars for style and comfort, while the rich buy cars for their company, because they are deductible. Again, this goes with secret number 3- get to know millionaires.

7: 10 Characteristic of Successful Entrepreneur

Entrepreneurs are Passionate, dedicated, and optimistic

1: Entrepreneurs Always Take Action – People who have a concept but   not a detailed strategy are more likely to have that special entrepreneurial ability. "Invent as you go, rather than spending too much time planning."

2: Many Entrepreneurs are insecure underneath just like most people. But this does not stop them from achieving their business goals.

3: Entrepreneurs are very crafty. It's not about having enough resources, but being resourceful with what you do have.

4: Entrepreneurs are fearless. While most people avoid risk, Entrepreneurs see potential. Most Entrepreneurs are optimists. They believe all their hard work and time invested will pay off at the end.

5: Most Entrepreneurs possess extraordinary energy. They have a positive attitude and confidence about them that makes them stand out.

6: Everything evolves. Nothing stays the same. Successful Entrepreneurs know when to evolve.

They constantly update their business according to customer feedbacks.

7: Entrepreneurs need to be comfortable with the process of evaluating their own performance.

8: Entrepreneurs are motivated by challenges. When confronted by adversity, Entrepreneurs rise to the occasion.

9: Entrepreneurs recover quickly. Successful Entrepreneurs fail often. If they fail, they resist the urge to mope or feel sorry for themselves. They move to the next big project immediately.

10: Entrepreneurs work hard. When they fall down, they pick themselves right back up until they get it right, no matter how long it takes.

You really can start a Business with little or No Money

You might be limited to a strict budget when you want to start your own business, but that doesn't mean you don't have options. It is very possible to start a business with very little money, work ethic, and marketing know-how. Here is list of 5 options you can use to start a business if you have little to no money.

1: *Make a physical product* - what you decide to make is up to you. There are several places where you can sell your handmade items online.

Abe's Market - Abe's Market sells everything organic. You can find health and nutritional products, face and body lotions, pet care, gifts, and a whole lot more.

Etsy – Etsy is another great place to find anything homemade. It's more of an arts and craft kind a store.

Bonanza – Bonanza is another homemade marketplace

ebay – ebay is one of the biggest online e-commerce marketplace in the world. It is user friendly and its customized listing option makes it a great choice for selling any household items.

2: *Resell Something* – If you don't want to make anything you can still grow a large business just by reselling already made products. You can do this by using variety of channels.

Drop Shipping – You can set up an online store and partner with a reliable drop shipping companies that will do the order fulfillment for you. Online e-commerce platform, Shopify, has a great drop shipping guide.

Thrift Stores and Garage Sales – If you know where to look you can find items at thrift stores, flea markets, and garage sales. You can resell them online or sell at your local community for a nice profit.

3: *Sell Your Services* – One way to start a business with little or no money is to sell your services instead of a physical product. There is a huge variety of services you can offer depending on your background and interests. You'll need a branding plan to make sure your name and company gets in front of the people who need your service. There are quite a few popular places where you can promote your product or services for free. Fiverr is probably the biggest and the best in my opinion. You can also visit craigslist, odesk, and elance. It's also useful to have a website to show examples of your work, list your experience, and blog about your industry.

4: *Barter to get what you need* – It's hard to start a business without any funds. However, there are ways to get what you need without money. For instance, if you need a used laptop, try to barter for it. You can offer babysitting or other services to your neighbor for their old Mac book.

5: Utilize Low cost services – Use sites like fiverr, craigslist and elance to advertise your product or service and build up your company. This is a great way to get branding materials, printed items, or other needed items without much cost. For additional savings, be sure to look for coupon codes such as retailmenot.com

Starting your own business requires ingenuity and a passion for what you are doing. Once you find yourself doing something you enjoy, you'll be more likely to find ways to make it all come together!

Conclusion

Let me ask you a question, do you know many people who have a large amount of money also wish you had a large amount of money? Sure, you may think the wealthy look down on the poor and like to rub their big fortune in their face, but this isn't always true.

There are plenty of people living in poverty right now. People who live in poverty are a mystery to the wealthy. They understand that money is available to anyone but they have to be persistent, motivated, and fully focused to be able to get it.

Take it from me – you may not think highly of yourself right now because of the situation you are in, but don't let that bring you down. You need to overcome your present situation, learn from your past and move forward.

More importantly, you need to realize that the only thing special about those self-made millionaires is the fact that they were willing to work long hours, were fully motivated, and they devoted a large amount of brain power into their work. Motivation, my friends, is the true key to becoming a successful entrepreneur.

May I ask a small favor from you? If you can find the time, can you please leave an honest review for this book? Whether it is good or bad, I would really appreciate it! I am always striving to improve my book.

Thank You!